THE PERFECT
$\mathcal{B}$ARBECUE
BOOK

THE PERFECT
ℬARBECUE
BOOK

LORENZ BOOKS

This edition published by Lorenz Books
27 West 20th Street, New York, NY 10011

LORENZ BOOKS are available for bulk purchase for sales promotion
and for premium use. For details, write or call the sales director,
Lorenz Books, 27 West 20th Street, New York, NY 10011;
(800) 354-9657

Lorenz Books is an imprint of
Anness Publishing Inc.

ISBN 0 7548 0657 X

Publisher: Joanna Lorenz
Editor: Sarah Ainley
Copy Editor: Jenni Fleetwood
Designers: Patrick McLeavey & Jo Brewer
Illustrator: Anna Koska
Photographers: Edward Allwright, Michell Garrett & Don Last
Recipes: Christine France, Steven Wheeler & Liz Trigg

Printed and bound in Singapore

Contents

Introduction

There can be no finer stimulus to the appetite than the sight and aroma of good food grilling on the barbecue, and no more relaxing way to entertain family and friends.

As with so many aspects of cooking, success depends as much on forethought as it does on flair. It is no use getting all fired up, only to find there's not enough fuel, or that you haven't bought any buns for the burgers. Good equipment is easy to acquire, enthusiasm is a ready commodity, but expertise is largely a matter of planning and practice.

What type of barbecue should you choose? The range is vast, from small disposable foil containers to state-of-the-art gas or electric cooking stations. If you are new to this style of cooking, start with a basic brazier or barbecue. The former is simply a firebox on legs, with vents or dampers to control the air flow to the burning coals, and a grill with a variable height. A basic barbecue is bowl-shaped, with a domed hood that reflects the heat and speeds up the cooking process, and can also act as a shield if rain threatens to put out your fire.

Both braziers and barbecues usually have wheels, plus one or two solid legs for anchorage. The advantage of this is that you can move the barbecue if the wind changes direction, a point to consider if you plan to build an outdoor cooking and eating area. Make sure the site is sheltered, handy to the house and away from vegetation. Locate the fire so the prevailing wind blows smoke away from the area.

The most efficient way to build a solid-fuel fire is to spread a 2-inch-deep layer of wood or lump charcoal on the grate, with more fuel piled up in a pyramid in the center. Squirt lighter fluid on the pyramid, light with a long match and let burn for 15 minutes before spreading out the coals. Don't start to cook until the coals are ash gray. This will take 30–45 minutes. (If you are using self-igniting charcoal, follow the manufacturer's instructions.)

Before starting to cook, make sure you have everything you need, including oven mitts, a sturdy flame-proof apron and a water-filled spray bottle for emergencies. Cooking time and temperature will vary according to the type and density of the food. Control the heat by raising or lowering the grill, or by bunching or spreading the coals. This is relatively easy when you are grilling a single item, such as a whole salmon, but cooking several different sorts of food simultaneously is more tricky: Create a hot spot for steaks, sausages and chops by pushing some of the coals together in the center, then place vegetables, delicate poultry and seafood around the rim, where the heat is less intense. Desserts such as baked bananas and glazed pineapple cook well on the dying embers.

Never be tempted to rush a barbecue. The enjoyment comes from the combination of great-tasting food and a relaxing setting, so take it slowly, steadily and safely, and have some fun!

7

Barbecue Favorites

BEEF

Use high heat for beef, cutting off excess fat to minimize flare-ups. Grill 1-inch steaks for 5 minutes if you like them rare, 8 minutes for medium and 12 minutes for well done. Burgers taste best when rare, but food-handling experts recommend cooking until well done. The juices should run clear and the flesh should not have any trace of pinkness.

CHICKEN

Always a popular choice, especially when marinated. Use low heat for breasts, medium for wings, drumsticks or quarters. Allow about 15 minutes for breasts and wings; 30 minutes for other cuts and cornish hens. Chicken must be thoroughly cooked; it is a good idea to precook chicken in the microwave or oven and then transfer it straight to the barbecue. Chicken should not be reheated once it has cooled.

FISH

Keep the heat low to medium. Cut slashes in whole fish to conduct the heat to the bone. Cook firm-fleshed varieties directly on the grill, but wrap delicate fish in foil, with lemon and butter. Oily fish bastes itself. Finish cooking over high heat to crisp the skin. Allow about 10 minutes per 1-inch thickness for whole fish over 5 pounds; as for smaller whole fish, steaks and fillets, the fish is ready when it flakes easily when tested with a sharp knife.

FRUIT

Bananas are ideal; just place them on the grill and they'll cook in their skins to tender perfection. Try pineapple and apples in foil, too.

LAMB

Cook steaks and chops over medium heat for 10–15 minutes; kebabs can take less time. A butterflied leg of lamb cooks very successfully in about an hour.

8

PORK

Fillet is great for kebabs. Cubes or chops 1 inch thick need about 15 minutes over medium heat. Spare ribs take 30–40 minutes, and thick sausages should be cooked in 15–20 minutes. All pork must be thoroughly cooked; start sausages off in the microwave, if desired.

SHELLFISH

Peeled shrimp and scallops are delicate, so keep the heat low and baste often. Shell-on crustaceans can take medium heat and will need slightly longer (as a rough guide, give large shrimp in the shell 6–8 minutes, peeled shrimp 4–6 minutes). Cook mussels until they open.

VEGETABLES

Wrap potatoes and squash in foil and cook them in the coals; cook mushrooms with herb butter in foil on the grill. Grilled eggplants, tomatoes, onions, peppers and zucchini taste superb. For timing, see individual recipes.

9

NOTE: All cooking times are approximate.

SAFETY TIPS

Make sure the barbecue is on level ground.
Never leave a fire unattended.
Keep children and animals away.
Never pour flammable liquid onto the barbecue.
Wear a flameproof apron and use mitts and long-handled tools.
Smother the fire after cooking.

Techniques

COOKING IN FOIL

Delicate foods, such as scallops or flounder fillets, are best cooked in oil on the grill rack. More robust items, such as potatoes and squash, can be wrapped in foil and placed in the coals themselves. To make a double layer for extra strength, cut 2 equal pieces of heavy-duty foil, large enough to wrap the food. Lightly grease the foil with melted butter or oil, then place the food in the center of the foil and add any flavorings or seasonings. Close packages securely, twisting the edges of the foil together so the juices cannot escape during cooking.

PREPARING WHOLE FISH

Small, oily fish, such as mackerel or trout, cook perfectly on the barbecue. Unless the fishmonger has already done so, cut off the fins and strip out the gills with kitchen scissors. Hold the fish firmly at the tail end and use the back of a small knife blade to remove the scales, scraping toward the head. Rinse well in cold water, then slit the fish from under the tail to behind the gills to open up the belly. Remove and discard the entrails and rinse the cavity thoroughly. Rub the cavity with salt and rinse again. Dry with paper towels.

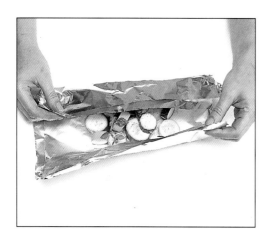

Marinating

Besides adding flavor and moisture, marinades tenderize foods, especially meat. Oil is usually included in a savory marinade, the amount governed by whether the food is lean or has a relatively high fat content. Arrange the food in a single layer, pour the marinade over it and turn the food to coat it evenly.

Cover and chill for the recommended time, turning occasionally. When cooking, baste with the remaining marinade, but be careful if it is high in oil or alcohol, as flare-ups can occur. Sweet marinades containing sugar or honey burn easily; brush them over the food toward the end of the cooking time.

Basic Marinade (for meat or fish)
Mix 1 crushed garlic clove with 3 tablespoons each sunflower oil and dry sherry. Stir in 1 tablespoon each Worcestershire sauce and dark soy sauce. Add a grinding of black pepper.

Herb Marinade (for fish or chicken)
Mix ½ cup dry white wine with ¼ cup olive oil and 1 tablespoon lemon juice. Add 2 tablespoons finely chopped fresh herbs and a grinding of black pepper.

Citrus Marinade (for duck or pork)
Mix 1 teaspoon each grated lemon, lime and orange rind with 2 tablespoons each lemon, lime and orange juice. Add 3 tablespoons sunflower oil, 2 tablespoons honey and 1 tablespoon soy sauce. Whisk in 1 teaspoon Dijon mustard.

Red Wine Marinade (for beef or game)
Mix ⅔ cup dry red wine with 1 tablespoon each olive oil and red wine vinegar, 3 crushed garlic cloves and 2 crumbled bay leaves.

11

Meats

Five-spice Ribs

INGREDIENTS

2¼ pounds Chinese-style spare ribs
½ teaspoon sweet chili sauce
¼ cup soy sauce
1 tablespoon sunflower oil
2 teaspoons Chinese five-spice powder
2 garlic cloves, crushed
1 tablespoon grated fresh ginger
3 tablespoons dark brown sugar
4 scallions, to serve

SERVES 4

1 If the spare ribs are still joined, either ask the butcher to separate them, or do it yourself with a sharp knife. Place the spare ribs in a large mixing bowl.

2 Mix the chili sauce, soy sauce and oil in a separate bowl. Stir in the five-spice powder, garlic, ginger and sugar. Mix well, then pour the mixture over the ribs. Turn the ribs to coat them thoroughly. Cover and marinate overnight in the refrigerator.

3 Cook the ribs on a medium-hot barbecue, turning frequently, for 30–40 minutes. Brush occasionally with the remaining marinade.

4 Slice the scallions. Serve the cooked spare ribs on a platter, with the scallions scattered on top.

COOK'S TIP

Make sure you buy authentic Chinese five-spice powder and not five-spice seasoning, which is much saltier.

Tex-Mex Burgers

INGREDIENTS

2½ cups lean ground beef
1 small onion, finely chopped
1 small green bell pepper, finely chopped
1 garlic clove, crushed
salt and ground black pepper
oil, for brushing
4 fresh flour tortillas
chopped fresh cilantro, to garnish
lettuce, to serve (optional)
GUACAMOLE
2 ripe avocados, halved and pitted
1 garlic clove, crushed
2 tomatoes, chopped
juice of 1 lime or lemon
½ small fresh green chili, seeded and chopped
2 tablespoons chopped fresh cilantro

SERVES 4

1 Combine the ground beef with the onion, bell pepper and garlic in a bowl. Add plenty of salt and pepper. Mix well, then divide the mixture into four portions.

2 Carefully shape each portion into a patty, using dampened hands or a burger press. Cover with a cloth and set aside while you make the guacamole.

3 Scoop the avocado flesh into a bowl and mash with a fork, then mix in the garlic, tomatoes, lime juice, chili and cilantro. Add salt and pepper to taste. Cover the surface of the guacamole with plastic wrap, leaving no air between plastic wrap and guacamole.

4 Brush the burgers lightly with oil. Grill on a medium-hot barbecue for 8–10 minutes, or until cooked through. Turn the burgers once during cooking.

5 Just before serving, heat the tortillas on the barbecue for about 15 seconds on each side. Place a spoonful of guacamole and a burger on each tortilla, then fold the tortilla over. Garnish with chopped cilantro and serve plain or with lettuce.

Peppered Steak in Beer & Garlic

INGREDIENTS

4 beef sirloin steaks, 1 inch thick, about 6
ounces each
2 garlic cloves, crushed
½ cup brown ale or stout
2 tablespoons dark brown sugar
2 tablespoons Worcestershire sauce
1 tablespoon corn oil
1 tablespoon crushed black peppercorns

SERVES 4

16

1 Place the steaks in a single layer in a shallow dish. Mix the garlic, ale, sugar, Worcestershire sauce and oil in a bowl. Pour the mixture over the meat, turn to coat evenly, then cover and marinate in the refrigerator for 2–3 hours or overnight.

2 Pour the marinade into a bowl and set aside. Sprinkle the peppercorns evenly over the steaks and press them into the surface.

3 Cook the steaks on a hot barbecue for 3–6 minutes per side or until done to your taste. Turn them once during cooking and use the reserved marinade  for basting. Serve each steak with a baked potato and a green salad, if desired.

COOK'S TIP
*Use the marinade sparingly, as the alcohol
will cause flare-ups if so much is used that
it drips onto the coals. Brush on a small
amount of marinade at a time.*

Racks of Lamb with Lavender Marinade

INGREDIENTS

4 racks of lamb, each with 3–4 chops
1 shallot, finely chopped
3 tablespoons chopped fresh lavender
1 tablespoon balsamic vinegar
2 tablespoons olive oil
1 tablespoon lemon juice
salt and ground black pepper
handful of lavender sprigs

SERVES 4

3 Scatter a few lavender sprigs over the grill rack or on the coals of a medium-hot barbecue. Lift the lamb out of the marinade and place it on the grill. Cook for 15–20 minutes or until golden brown on the outside and slightly pink in the center. Baste occasionally with the remaining marinade. Serve the lamb hot, garnished with more lavender sprigs.

VARIATION

Use rosemary sprigs instead of lavender, if you prefer. They release a wonderful aroma when burned on the barbecue.

17

1 Place the racks of lamb in a large bowl or wide dish and sprinkle the chopped shallot on top. Crumble the lavender between your fingers to release the scent and distribute it over the lamb.

2 Combine the vinegar, oil and lemon juice in a small bowl. Whisk with a fork, then pour over the lamb. Sprinkle the lamb with salt and pepper to taste, and turn to coat evenly.

Bacon Kofta Kebabs with Bulgur Salad

INGREDIENTS

½ pound lean bacon, chopped
1 small onion, chopped
1 celery stick, chopped
5 tablespoons fresh whole-wheat bread crumbs
3 tablespoons chopped fresh thyme
2 tablespoons Worcestershire sauce
beaten egg, to bind
salt and ground black pepper
oil, for brushing
BULGUR SALAD
⅔ cup bulgur
¼ cup toasted sunflower seeds
2 tablespoons olive oil
handful of celery leaves, chopped

SERVES 4

1 Soak 8 bamboo skewers in cold water for 30 minutes. Place the bacon, onion, celery and bread crumbs in a food processor. Process until finely chopped. Add the thyme and Worcestershire sauce, with salt and pepper to taste. Process briefly. With the motor running, add just enough beaten egg to bind the mixture.

2 Using a knife, scrape the bacon mixture onto a board, then, with dampened hands, divide the mixture into 8 equal portions. Drain the bamboo skewers and shape each portion of bacon mixture into a long sausage, molding and pressing it onto a skewer. Chill the kofta kebabs in the refrigerator while you make the bulgur salad.

3 Place the bulgur in a large bowl. Pour boiling water over it to cover. Let stand for 30 minutes or until the grains are tender, then transfer to a sieve lined with cheesecloth or a clean dish towel. Drain well, then gather up the sides of the cloth and squeeze out as much liquid as possible from the bulgur. Transfer to a serving bowl.

4 Add the sunflower seeds and oil to the bowl, with salt and ground black pepper to taste. Stir in the chopped celery leaves and set the salad aside.

5 Cook the kofta kebabs over a medium-hot barbecue for 8–10 minutes, brushing with oil and turning occasionally to ensure that they are cooked through. Serve the kofta kebabs on the skewers, accompanied by the bulgur salad.

Mixed Grill Skewers with Horseradish Butter

INGREDIENTS

4 small lamb noisettes, about 1 inch thick
4 lamb kidneys
8 strips bacon
8 cherry tomatoes
8 chipolata sausages
20 bay leaves
HORSERADISH BUTTER
3 tablespoons butter
2 tablespoons prepared horseradish
salt and ground black pepper

SERVES 4

20

1 Trim any excess fat from the lamb noisettes. Cut the kidneys in half and remove the cores with scissors. Cut each strip of bacon in half crosswise then wrap each piece around a tomato or a half-kidney.

2 Carefully thread the lamb noisettes, chipolatas, bay leaves and wrapped tomatoes and kidneys onto four long metal skewers. Spear the meat  through the side to present the largest possible area to the heat.

3 Melt the butter in a small pan. Stir in the horseradish. Brush a little of the mixture over the skewered meats and sprinkle with salt and pepper.

4 Grill the skewers on a medium-hot barbecue for 12–15 minutes, turning occasionally, until all the ingredients are cooked through. Keep the rest of the horseradish butter warm by setting the pan on the edge of the grill. Pour it over the skewers to serve.

VARIATION
Use cubes of pork instead of kidneys, if you prefer. Mushrooms and baby onions would make a good addition.

Grilled Sausages with Prunes & Bacon

INGREDIENTS

8 large, meaty pork sausages
2 tablespoons Dijon mustard
24 pitted prunes
8 strips bacon

SERVES 4

1 With a sharp knife, make a long slit along one side of each sausage, cutting about three-quarters of the way through, so that each sausage can be opened out to make a long, narrow pocket.

2 Spread the cut surface of each pocket with mustard, then place three prunes in the middle of each sausage, pressing them down firmly to secure.

3 Using the back of a knife, stretch the strips of bacon out thinly, then wrap a strip around each filled sausage to hold its shape. Use toothpicks (soaked in water to prevent scorching) to secure the bacon, if necessary.

4 Grill the wrapped sausages over a hot barbecue for 15–18 minutes, turning occasionally, until evenly browned and cooked through.

COOK'S TIP
Specialty butchers pride themselves on selling a wide variety of flavored sausages. Vary this recipe with venison sausages, or try pork sausages with apple.

21

Pork & Pineapple Satay

INGREDIENTS

1 pound pork shoulder (boneless)
1 small onion, chopped
1 garlic clove, chopped
¼ cup soy sauce
finely grated rind of ½ lemon
1 teaspoon ground cumin
1 teaspoon ground coriander
1 teaspoon ground turmeric
1 teaspoon dark brown sugar
1 can (8 ounces) pineapple chunks, drained
SATAY SAUCE
¾ cup canned unsweetened coconut milk
6 tablespoons crunchy peanut butter
1 garlic clove, crushed
2 teaspoons soy sauce
1 teaspoon dark brown sugar

SERVES 4

1 Soak 4 long or 8 short bamboo skewers in water for 30 minutes. Trim any fat from the pork and cut it into 1-inch cubes. Place the meat in a large bowl.

2 Combine the onion, garlic, soy sauce, lemon rind, spices and sugar in a food processor. Add 2 pineapple chunks and process the mixture to a fairly smooth paste.

Scrape the paste into the bowl containing the pork. Toss to coat evenly.

3 Make the sauce. Pour the coconut milk into a small saucepan. Stir in the peanut butter, then add the garlic, soy sauce and sugar. Heat gently, and stir until

smooth and hot. Cover the pan and keep hot on the edge of the barbecue.

4 Drain the skewers and thread them with alternating pieces of pork and pineapple. Grill on a medium-hot barbecue for 10–12 minutes, turning occasionally, until the pork is cooked through. Serve immediately, with the satay sauce.

22

Poultry

Chicken & Citrus Kebabs

INGREDIENTS

4 skinless, boneless chicken breasts
fresh mint sprigs and 4 twists each of
lime and lemon, to garnish
MARINADE
finely grated rind and juice of ½ orange
finely grated rind and juice of
½ small lemon or lime
2 tablespoons olive oil
2 tablespoons honey
2 tablespoons chopped fresh mint
¼ teaspoon ground cumin
salt and ground black pepper

SERVES 4

2 Lift the chicken cubes out of the marinade and thread onto metal skewers. Grill on a medium-hot barbecue for 15 minutes, basting occasionally with the marinade. Turn the skewers frequently.

3 Garnish the kebabs with mint sprigs and citrus twists. Serve with a side salad, if desired.

1 Cut the chicken into 1-inch cubes. To make the marinade, mix the grated citrus rind and juice in a bowl, then stir in the olive oil, honey, mint and cumin. Add the chicken cubes and stir to coat. Cover and marinate for at least 2 hours.

COOK'S TIP
Chicken breasts are tender and will dry out over an intense fire. Cook them on the edge of the barbecue or wait until the coals are cooler.

25

Deep South Salad

INGREDIENTS

4 ears fresh corn
4 skinless, boneless chicken breasts
1 tablespoons corn oil
½ pound bacon
3 tablespoons butter, softened
4 ripe bananas
4 firm tomatoes, halved
1 head butter lettuce or escarole,
separated into leaves
1 bunch watercress, trimmed
ground black pepper
DRESSING
5 peanut oil
1 tablespoon white wine vinegar
2 teaspoons maple syrup
2 teaspoons mild mustard
1 tablespoon water

SERVES 4

1 Make the dressing by whisking all the ingredients in a bowl. Set aside. Peel back the corn husks, remove the silky threads, then fold the husks back over the kernels. Parboil the corn in a large saucepan of lightly salted water for about 15 minutes, until the kernels are just tender.

2 Meanwhile, brush the chicken breasts with oil, season them lightly with ground black pepper and grill on a medium-hot barbecue for 15 minutes or until  cooked through, turning once. Barbecue the bacon for 8–10 minutes, until crisp.

3 Drain the corn, brush the kernels with butter, and barbecue, along with the whole peeled bananas and tomatoes, until lightly browned.

4 Whisk the dressing again and add the salad leaves. Toss lightly and arrange them on four large plates. Slice the hot chicken breasts and arrange them  on the salad leaves with the bacon, bananas, tomatoes and grilled corn.

Blackened Cajun Chicken & Corn

INGREDIENTS

8 chicken pieces
2 whole ears corn
2 teaspoons garlic salt
2 teaspoons ground black pepper
1½ teaspoons ground cumin
1½ teaspoons paprika
1 teaspoons cayenne pepper
3 tablespoons butter, melted
chopped parsley, to garnish

SERVES 4

1 Cut any excess fat from the chicken, but leave the skin on. Make several deep slashes in the fleshiest parts, to allow the flavors to penetrate.

2 Pull off the corn husks and remove the silky threads, then cut each ear into thick slices.

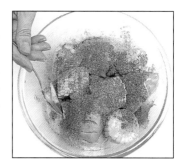

3 Mix the seasonings and spices in a small bowl. Brush the chicken and corn with melted butter and sprinkle the spices over them. Toss well to coat evenly.

4 Grill the chicken pieces on a medium-hot barbecue for 10 minutes, turning occasionally. Add the corn and grill for 15 more minutes, until the chicken has begun to blacken, and the corn is lightly charred. Garnish with parsley and serve.

COOK'S TIP
Chicken wings cook more quickly than other pieces; if you use wings, grill them alongside the corn for the same amount of time.

28

Barbecued Turkey Rolls with Gazpacho Sauce

INGREDIENTS

4 turkey cutlets
1 tablespoon red pesto (made with
sun-dried tomatoes)
4 chorizo sausages
salt and ground black pepper
GAZPACHO SAUCE
1 green bell pepper, seeded and chopped
1 red bell pepper, seeded and chopped
3-inch piece cucumber, roughly chopped
1 tomato, roughly chopped
1 garlic clove, roughly chopped
1 tablespoon red wine vinegar
3 tablespoons olive oil

SERVES 4

1 Make the sauce. Combine the bell peppers, cucumber, tomato and garlic in a food processor. Add the vinegar, with 2 tablespoons of the oil. Process until almost smooth. Scrape into a bowl, season with salt and pepper and set aside.

2 If the turkey cutlets are quite thick, place them between two sheets of plastic wrap and flatten them slightly by pressing them firmly with a rolling pin.

3 Spread the pesto over each flattened turkey breast, add a chorizo and roll up firmly. Slice the rolls thickly, then spear them onto 4 long metal skewers. The turkey rolls

should be speared though the side, so they present the largest possible area to the heat.

4 Grill on a medium-hot barbecue for 10–12 minutes, turning once. Serve immediately, with the gazpacho sauce.

Sweet & Sour Kebabs

INGREDIENTS

2 skinless, boneless chicken breasts
8 baby onions
4 strips bacon
2 large, firm bananas
1 red pepper, seeded and cut into
1-inch squares
MARINADE
2 tablespoons light brown sugar
1 tablespoon Worcestershire sauce
2 tablespoons lemon juice
salt and ground black pepper
HARLEQUIN RICE
2 tablespoons olive oil
4 cups cooked rice (about 1 cup raw)
1 cup cooked peas
1 small red bell pepper, seeded and diced

SERVES 4

1 Make the marinade by mixing all the ingredients in a bowl. Cut each chicken breast into four pieces and add to the marinade. Toss to coat, then cover and marinate in the refrigerator for at least 4 hours, preferably overnight.

2 Bring a small saucepan of water to a boil. Add the onions to the pan and blanch for 5 minutes. Drain and set aside. Cut each strip of bacon in half crosswise. Peel the bananas and cut each one into 4 pieces. Wrap a piece of bacon around each chunk of banana.

3 Lift the chicken pieces out of the marinade and thread them onto long metal skewers with the baby onions, bacon-wrapped banana chunks and pepper squares. Brush the kebabs with the marinade.

4 Grill on a low-to-medium-hot barbecue for 15 minutes, turning frequently and basting the kebabs with the marinade. Move to the edge of the barbecue to keep warm while you prepare the rice.

5 Heat the oil in a pan. Add the rice, peas and pepper and heat through. Serve with the kebabs.

Spiced Chicken Breasts with Coconut Sauce

INGREDIENTS

1 block (7 ounces) creamed coconut, cubed
1¼ cups boiling water
3 garlic cloves, chopped
2 scallions, chopped
1 fresh green chili, chopped
3 tablespoons grated fresh ginger
1 teaspoon fennel seeds
½ teaspoon black peppercorns
seeds from 4 green cardamom pods
2 tablespoons ground coriander
1 teaspoon ground cumin
1 teaspoon grated nutmeg
½ teaspoon ground cloves
½ teaspoon ground turmeric
4 large skinless, boneless chicken breasts
onion rings and fresh cilantro
sprigs, to garnish

SERVES 4

1 Dissolve the coconut in the boiling water in a heatproof pitcher. Combine the garlic, scallions, chili, ginger and all the spices in a food processor or blender. Add the coconut mixture and process to a smooth paste.

2 Slash the chicken breasts in several places. Arrange them in a single layer in a shallow dish. Spoon half the coconut mixture over them and toss to coat evenly. Cover and marinate for 30 minutes at room temperature, or overnight in the fridge.

3 Heat the remaining coconut mixture gently in a pan, stirring constantly, then keep it warm at the edge of the barbecue. Drain the chicken breasts and grill them over low-to-medium heat for 12–15 minutes, turning once, until fully cooked. Garnish with onion rings and fresh cilantro sprigs. Serve with the coconut sauce.

Chicken with Herb & Ricotta Stuffing

INGREDIENTS

¼ cup ricotta cheese
1 garlic clove, crushed
3 tablespoons chopped
fresh herbs (chives, flat leaf parsley
and mint)
2 tablespoons fresh brown bread crumbs
salt and freshly ground black pepper
8 chicken drumsticks
8 strips bacon
1 teaspoon wholegrain mustard
1 tablespoons sunflower oil
lettuce, to serve (optional)

SERVES 4

33

1 Make the stuffing. Mix the ricotta cheese with the garlic, herbs and bread crumbs in a bowl. Season the mixture well with plenty of salt and black pepper.

2 Carefully loosen the skin from each drumstick and spoon a little of the herb stuffing under each, smoothing the skin back firmly.

3 Wrap a strip of bacon around the wide end of each drumstick, to secure the skin over the stuffing.

4 Mix the mustard and oil in a bowl, then brush the mixture over the chicken. Cook on a medium-hot barbecue for 20–25 minutes, turning occasionally, until the chicken is cooked through. Serve with lettuce, if desired.

Fish & Seafood

Char~grilled Tuna with Fiery Pepper Paste

INGREDIENTS

4 tuna steaks, about 6 ounces each
juice and finely grated rind of 1 lime
2 tablespoons olive oil
salt and ground black pepper
lime wedges, to serve
PEPPER PASTE
2 red bell peppers, seeded and halved
1 small onion
2 garlic cloves, crushed
2 fresh red chilies, sliced
1 slice of white bread without crust, diced
3 tablespoons olive oil, plus extra for brushing

SERVES 4

1 Trim any skin from the tuna. Place the steaks in a single layer in a shallow dish. Sprinkle on the lime juice and rind, olive oil, salt and pepper. Cover and chill until needed.

2 Make the pepper paste. Brush the peppers with oil and grill, skin side down, on a hot barbecue, until the skin blisters and blackens. Cook the unpeeled onion on the barbecue, turning occasionally, until the skin starts to blacken and the flesh softens.

3 Put the peppers and onion in a bowl, cover with paper towels and cool for 10 minutes, then remove the skins. Process the onion and pepper flesh with the garlic, chilies, bread and oil until smooth. (Remove the seeds from the chilies beforehand if you prefer a milder flavor.) Scrape into a bowl and add salt to taste.

4 Lift the tuna steaks from the marinade and grill them on a hot barbecue for 8–10 minutes. Serve with the pepper paste and lime wedges.

Mexican Barbecued Salmon

INGREDIENTS

1 small red onion
1 garlic clove
6 plum tomatoes
2 tablespoons butter
3 tablespoons ketchup
2 tablespoons Dijon mustard
2 tablespoons dark brown sugar
1 tablespoon honey
1 teaspoon cayenne pepper
1 tablespoon ancho chili powder
1 tablespoon paprika
1 tablespoons Worcestershire sauce
4 salmon fillets, about 6 ounces each
fresh cilantro sprigs, to garnish

SERVES 4

1 Finely chop the red onion and garlic and mix them in a bowl. Dice the tomatoes and keep them separate from the onion mixture.

2 Melt the butter in a large, heavy saucepan. Add the onion and garlic and cook for 8–10 minutes. Add the tomatoes and simmer for 15 minutes.

3 Stir in the ketchup, mustard, brown sugar, honey, spices and Worcestershire sauce. Mix well. Bring to a boil, lower the heat and simmer for 20 minutes. Puree the mixture in a food processor, then scrape into a bowl and let cool.

4 Arrange the salmon fillets on a plate and brush them with the sauce. Cover and chill for at least 2 hours. Grill over a medium-hot barbecue for 2–3 minutes on each side. Garnish with fresh cilantro sprigs and serve with any remaining sauce.

COOK'S TIP
Try the sauce with barbecued sausages or as a hamburger relish. It would also make a good alternative marinade for the tiger shrimp skewers in this book.

Tiger Shrimp with Walnut Pesto

INGREDIENTS

12–16 large tiger shrimp, in the shell
WALNUT PESTO
½ cup walnut pieces
¼ cup chopped fresh flat-leaf parsley
¼ cup shredded fresh basil
2 garlic cloves, chopped
3 tablespoons grated Parmesan cheese
2 tablespoons extra virgin olive oil
2 tablespoons walnut oil
salt and ground black pepper

SERVES 4

38

1 Peel the shrimp. Remove the heads, but leave the tails intact. Remove the veins. Put the shrimp in a large bowl, cover and set aside while you make the pesto.

2 Combine the walnuts, parsley, basil, garlic and Parmesan in a food processor. Add both types of oil and grind to a paste. Scrape the paste into a bowl and season with salt and pepper.

3 Add half the pesto to the shrimp. Toss to coat; replace the cover. Marinate for about an hour at room temperature, or overnight in the refrigerator.

4 Soak 8 short bamboo skewers in cold water for 30 minutes. Drain and thread with the shrimp. Cook on a medium-hot barbecue for 4–6 minutes. Serve with the remaining pesto.

Barbecued Stuffed Calamari

INGREDIENTS

1¼ pounds baby squid
1 garlic clove, crushed
3 plum tomatoes, peeled and chopped
8 drained sun-dried tomatoes in oil, chopped
¼ cup shredded fresh basil,
plus extra to serve
¼ cup fresh white bread crumbs
1 tablespoon red wine vinegar
3 tablespoons olive oil
salt and ground black pepper
lemon juice, to serve

SERVES 4

3 Fill the squid with the stuffing, closing the ends with the toothpicks. Brush with the remaining 1 tablespoon oil and grill over a medium-hot

barbecue for 4–5 minutes, turning frequently. Sprinkle with lemon juice and extra basil to serve.

1 Prepare each squid by holding the body in one hand and gently pulling away the head and tentacles. Discard the head; chop the tentacles roughly. Keeping the body sac whole, remove the transparent "quill" from inside, then peel off the brown skin on the outside. Rub a little salt into each squid and wash well under cold water.

2 Mix the chopped squid, garlic, plum tomatoes, sun-dried tomatoes, basil and bread crumbs in a bowl. Stir in the vinegar, with 2 tablespoons of the oil. Season with plenty of salt and pepper and mix well. Soak toothpicks (as many as there are squid) in water for 10 minutes, then drain.

Grilled Sardines with Herb Salsa

INGREDIENTS

12–16 fresh sardines, cleaned
oil, for brushing
juice of 1 lemon
HERB SALSA
1 tablespoon butter
4 scallions, chopped
1 garlic clove, crushed
2 tablespoons finely chopped fresh parsley
2 tablespoons finely snipped fresh chives
2 tablespoons finely shredded fresh basil
2 tablespoons green-olive paste
2 teaspoons balsamic vinegar
grated rind of 1 lemon
salt and ground black pepper

SERVES 4

1 Rinse the sardines and dry them thoroughly with paper towels. Arrange the fish on a grill rack or on one half of a hinged grill.

2 Make the herb salsa. Melt the butter in a saucepan. Add the scallions and garlic and cook over low heat for 2 minutes, shaking the pan occasionally, until softened but not browned.

3 Stir in the herbs, olive paste, vinegar and lemon rind. Season to taste. Mix well. Cover the pan and keep it warm on the edge of the barbecue.

4 Brush the sardines lightly with oil. Sprinkle with lemon juice, salt and pepper. Grill over a medium-hot barbecue for 2 minutes on each side. Serve with  the warm salsa and offer chunks of crusty bread for mopping up the tasty juices.

Thai Spiced Fish

INGREDIENTS

4 red snapper or mullet, about ¾ pound each,
cleaned and scaled
banana leaves or heavy-duty foil, for wrapping
1 lime, halved
1 garlic clove, thinly sliced
2 scallions, thinly sliced
2 tablespoons Thai red curry paste
¼ cup coconut milk

SERVES 4

41

1 Cut several deep slashes in the side of each fish. Place each fish on a layer of banana leaves or a piece of foil large enough to enclose it. Slice one lime half and tuck the slices into the slashes in the fish, with slivers of garlic. Scatter the scallions over the fish.

2 Grate the rind and squeeze the juice from the remaining half-lime. Combine both in a bowl and stir in the curry paste and coconut milk. Mix well, then spoon evenly over the fish.

3 Wrap the leaves over the fish to enclose each one completely. Tie firmly with string. Grill on a medium-hot barbecue for 15–20 minutes, turning occasion-

ally. Check one portion to make sure the fish is thoroughly cooked, then serve all the fish in their wrappings, inviting guests to open them at the table.

Barbecued Scallops with Fennel & Lime

INGREDIENTS

1 fennel bulb
2 limes
12 large scallops
1 egg yolk
6 tablespoons butter, melted
oil, for brushing
salt and ground black pepper

SERVES 4

42

1 Trim any feathery leaves from the fennel and set them aside. Slice the fennel bulb lengthwise into thick wedges. Cut one lime into wedges. Grate the

rind of the remaining lime, then squeeze the juice.

2 Put the scallops in a bowl and add half the lime juice and half the grated rind. Toss to coat. Put the remaining lime rind and juice in a separate bowl. Add the egg yolk and whisk until pale and smooth.

3 Gradually whisk in the melted butter and continue whisking until the sauce is thick and smooth. Finely chop the reserved fennel leaves and stir them in, with salt and pepper to taste.

4 Brush the fennel wedges with oil. Cook them on a hot barbecue for 3–4 minutes, turning once. Add the scallops (placing them on a cooler area of the grill) and cook for 3–4 more minutes, turning once. Garnish with the lime wedges and serve with the lime and fennel sauce.

COOK'S TIP
If you can only obtain small scallops, use
16–20 size and thread them on flat skewers
so they can be turned more easily.

Vegetables & Vegetarian Dishes

Potato Skewers with Mustard Dip

INGREDIENTS

2½ pounds small new potatoes
7 ounces shallots, halved
2 tablespoons olive oil
1 tablespoon sea salt
MUSTARD DIP
4 garlic cloves, crushed
2 egg yolks
2 tablespoons lemon juice
1¼ cups extra-virgin
olive oil
2 teaspoons whole-grain mustard
salt and ground black pepper

SERVES 4

3 Brush the potatoes and shallots with oil and sprinkle with a little sea salt. Cook for 10–12 minutes over a hot barbecue, turning occasionally, until the potatoes and shallots are tender. Serve immediately, with the mustard dip.

1 Make the dip. Combine the garlic, egg yolks and lemon juice in a blender or food processor. Process for a few seconds until smooth. With the motor running, add the oil very gradually, pouring it through the cap or feeder tube in a thin stream, until the mixture forms a thick, glossy cream. Add the mustard and season with salt and pepper.

2 Bring a large saucepan of lightly salted water to a boil. Add the potatoes and parboil them for 5 minutes. Drain well, then thread with the shallots onto four metal skewers.

Red Bean & Mushroom Burgers

INGREDIENTS

1 tablespoon olive oil
1 small onion, finely chopped
1 garlic clove, crushed
1 teaspoon ground cumin
1 teaspoon ground coriander
½ teaspoon ground turmeric
1 cup finely chopped mushrooms
1 can (14 ounces) red kidney beans
2 tablespoons chopped fresh cilantro
whole-wheat flour (optional)
olive oil, for brushing
salt and ground black pepper
warmed pita bread, lettuce and
cherry tomatoes, to serve

SERVES 4

1 Heat the oil in a wide, shallow pan. Fry the onion and garlic over medium heat for about 5 minutes, until softened. Add the spices and cook for 1 more minute, stirring constantly.

2 Add the mushrooms. Raise the heat and cook for about 7 minutes, stirring frequently, until they are tender and dry. Remove the pan from the heat.

3 Drain the beans, transfer them to a bowl and mash with a fork. Add to the mushroom mixture, with the fresh cilantro, mixing thoroughly. Season with plenty of salt and pepper.

4 With floured hands, form the mixture into four flat burgers. If the mixture is too sticky to handle, mix in a little whole-wheat flour. Brush the burgers lightly with oil and cook on a hot barbecue for 8–10 minutes, turning once, until golden brown. Season to taste. These burgers are not as firm as meat burgers, so handle them gently on the barbecue. Serve with warmed pita bread, lettuce and cherry tomatoes. A spoonful of plain yogurt makes a welcome addition.

46

Grilled Eggplant & Feta Rolls

INGREDIENTS

2 large eggplants
salt
olive oil
10–12 drained sun-dried tomatoes in oil
handful of large, fresh basil leaves
scant 1 cup feta cheese
ground black pepper
fresh basil sprigs, to garnish

48

1 Slice the eggplants lengthwise into ¼-inch slices. Sprinkle with salt and layer in a colander. Let drain for about 30 minutes.

2 Rinse the eggplants under cold running water, drain and pat dry with paper towels. Brush both sides of each slice with oil. Grill on a hot barbecue for 2–3 minutes, turning once, until tender and golden brown.

3 Arrange the sun-dried tomatoes over one end of each eggplant slice. Add the fresh basil leaves. Cut the feta cheese into short sticks and place on top. Season with salt and ground black pepper.

4 Roll the eggplant slices up to enclose the filling. Cook the rolls on the barbecue for 2–3 minutes, until heated through. Garnish with fresh basil sprigs and serve with slices of ciabatta or whole-wheat bread.

VARIATION
Use tofu instead of feta cheese, if desired. For extra flavor, sprinkle the tofu with a little soy sauce before wrapping.

Brie Parcels with Almonds

INGREDIENTS

4 large grape leaves in brine, drained
½ pound of Brie cheese
2 tablespoons snipped fresh chives
¼ cup ground almonds
1 teaspoon crushed black peppercorns
1 tablespoon olive oil, plus extra for brushing
2 tablespoons sliced almonds

SERVES 2–4

3 Bring the stem end of each grape leaf up over the filling, then fold in the sides and top to enclose the filling completely and make a neat package. Brush the

packages with oil and cook on a hot barbecue for 3–4 minutes, until the cheese has begun to melt. Serve immediately, with crusty bread.

49

1 Rinse the grape leaves under cold water. Drain and dry on sheets of paper towels. Spread the leaves out on a board. Cut the Brie into four chunks and

place each chunk on a grape leaf.

2 Mix the fresh chives, ground almonds, peppercorns and oil in a bowl. Place a spoonful of the mixture over the Brie on each leaf. Sprinkle with the sliced almonds.

Grilled Mediterranean Vegetables

INGREDIENTS

2 eggplants
salt
2 large zucchini
1 red bell pepper
1 yellow bell pepper
1 fennel bulb
1 red onion
olive oil, for brushing
ground black pepper
SAUCE
⅔ cup plain yogurt
3 tablespoons pesto

SERVES 4

COOK'S TIP

*Baby vegetables are perfect for cooking on
the barbecue. If using baby eggplants,
simply slice them in half lengthwise.
They do not need to be salted.*

1 Cut the eggplants into ½-inch rounds. Sprinkle with salt and layer in a colander. Let drain for about 30 minutes, then rinse well under cold water, drain and pat dry with paper towels.

2 Cut the zucchini in half lengthwise. Cut the bell peppers in half, leaving the stalks on. Remove the seeds. Slice the fennel and onion into thick wedges.

3 Make the sauce by swirling the yogurt and pesto together to create a marbled effect. Spoon the sauce into a serving bowl.

4 Arrange the vegetables on the hot barbecue. Brush with oil and sprinkle with salt and pepper. Grill until lightly browned, turning occasionally. The eggplants and peppers will take 6–8 minutes to cook; the onion and fennel 4–5 minutes. Serve with the marbled pesto sauce.

Grilled Herb Polenta with Tomatoes

INGREDIENTS

olive oil, for dish
3 cups vegetable stock or water
1 teaspoon salt (optional)
1 cup polenta
2 tablespoons butter
5 tablespoons chopped fresh herbs (parsley,
chives and basil), plus extra to garnish
ground black pepper
4 large plum or beefsteak tomatoes, halved
salt

SERVES 4

1 Prepare the polenta several hours before you plan to have the barbecue. Grease a shallow baking dish lightly with oil and set it aside. Pour the stock into a large saucepan, add salt if needed, and bring to a boil. Lower the heat and add the polenta, stirring constantly.

2 Continue to stir over medium heat for 5 minutes, until the polenta thickens and starts to come away from the sides of the pan. Remove from the heat and stir in the butter and herbs, with black pepper to taste.

3 Transfer the mixture to the prepared baking dish and spread it out evenly. Let stand until the mixture has cooled and set. Turn out the polenta and stamp out rounds with a cookie cutter.

4 Brush the tomato halves with olive oil and sprinkle with salt and ground black pepper. Grill the tomatoes and polenta rounds on a moderately hot barbecue for 5 minutes, turning once. Garnish with the chopped fresh herbs and serve immediately.

Baked Squash with Parmesan

INGREDIENTS

*2 acorn or butternut squash,
1 pound each
1 tablespoon olive oil
salt and ground black pepper
4 tablespoons butter, softened
1 cup grated Parmesan cheese, plus extra
to serve
4 tablespoons pine nuts, toasted
½ teaspoon grated nutmeg*

SERVES 4

1 Cut the squash in half. Scoop out the seeds and rinse the flesh with cold water. Brush the cut surfaces with oil and sprinkle the flesh with salt and pepper.

2 Wrap each squash in a double layer of heavy-duty foil and place in the embers of the barbecue. Cook for 25–30 minutes or until tender, turning occasionally to ensure that the squash cook evenly.

3 Carefully lift the squash out of the embers and unwrap them. Scoop the flesh out into a bowl, keeping the shells intact. Dice the flesh, then stir in the softened

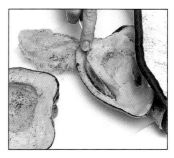

butter, Parmesan and pine nuts, with salt and pepper to taste.

4 Spoon the mixture back into the squash shells, sprinkle with any remaining Parmesan and the grated nutmeg, and serve immediately.

53

Desserts

Pineapple Wedges with Rum Butter Glaze

INGREDIENTS

1 pineapple
2 tablespoons dark brown sugar
1 teaspoon ground ginger
4 tablespoons butter, melted
2 tablespoons dark rum

SERVES 4

1 Soak 4 bamboo skewers in cold water for 30 minutes. Using a large, sharp knife, cut the pineapple in half, and then in half again, to make four wedges, each with a section of stalk and leaves. Cut out and discard the core from each wedge.

2 Cut between the flesh and skin to release the flesh without actually lifting it away. Leaving the flesh on the skin, slice it across into chunks. Drain the skewers,  then push each skewer lengthwise through a pineapple wedge and into the stalk, to hold the chunks in place.

3 Mix the sugar, ginger, melted butter and rum in a cup or bowl. Brush some of the the mixture on the pineapple. Grill on a hot barbecue for 3–4 minutes. Serve on individual plates, with the remaining rum mixture poured over.

COOK'S TIP
For an easier version, remove the skin and cut the pineapple into thick rounds. Remove the cores with an apple corer.

Grilled Apples on Cinnamon Toasts

INGREDIENTS

4 apples
juice of ½ lemon
2 tablespoons golden sugar
1 teaspoon ground cinnamon
4 individual brioches or muffins
¼ cup butter, melted
plain yogurt, to serve

SERVES 4

56

1 Core the apples, but do not peel them. Cut each apple horizontally into 3 or 4 rings and place in a shallow dish. Sprinkle lemon juice over the rings. Mix the sugar and cinnamon in a small bowl and set aside.

2 Cut the brioches into thick slices. Brush them with melted butter on both sides, then place them on a hot barbecue with the apple rings. Cook for 3–4 minutes, until the apples are cooked through and the brioches are toasted.

3 Sprinkle half the cinnamon sugar evenly over the cooked apple rings and toasted brioche slices, and cook for 1 more minute, until the topping turns a rich golden brown.

4 Arrange the apple rings on top of the toasted brioche slices to serve. Sprinkle with the rest of the cinnamon sugar on and add a generous spoonful of plain yogurt. Serve immediately.

Baked Bananas with Vanilla Butter

INGREDIENTS

4 bananas, unpeeled
seeds from 6 green cardamom pods
1 vanilla bean
finely grated rind of 1 small orange
2 tablespoons brandy or orange juice
¼ cup light brown sugar
3 tablespoons butter, melted
crème fraîche or plain yogurt, to serve

SERVES 4

58

1 Place the bananas, in their skins, on the hot barbecue. Let sit for 6–8 minutes, turning occasionally, until the skins are blackened all over.

2 Meanwhile, place the cardamom seeds in a mortar and crush lightly with a pestle. Split the vanilla bean lengthwise and scrape the tiny seeds into the mortar. Grind lightly, then mix in the orange rind, brandy or orange juice, sugar and butter, to make a thick paste.

3 Slit the skin of each banana, open out slightly, and spoon in a little of the spiced vanilla butter. Serve immediately, with a generous spoonful of crème fraîche or plain yogurt.

VARIATIONS
Children love these with maple syrup or melted chocolate instead of vanilla butter. For their parents, try drizzling liqueur over the bananas.

Nectarines with Marzipan & Mascarpone

INGREDIENTS

4 firm, ripe nectarines or peaches
3 ounces marzipan
5 tablespoons mascarpone cheese
3 macaroons, crushed

SERVES 4

3 Place the filled nectarine halves on a hot barbecue. Cook for 3–5 minutes, until they are hot and the mascarpone has begun to melt. Serve immediately.

VARIATIONS

Marzipan makes the perfect filling for barbecued fruits. It softens as it cooks and flavors the fruit beautifully. Try it as a filling for baked apples: mix in a little confectioners' sugar and some golden raisins, fill the apples and top each one with a few pieces of butter. Wrap in heavy-duty foil and bake for about 20 minutes on a medium-hot barbecue.

1 Cut the nectarines in half and remove the pits. Cut the marzipan into 8 pieces. Use your hands to press one piece into the cavity left in each nectarine half.

2 Spoon the mascarpone cheese on top of the marzipan pieces. Then sprinkle the crushed macaroons over the mascarpone.

59

Oranges in Cointreau & Maple Syrup

INGREDIENTS

2 tablespoons butter, melted, plus
extra for cooking
4 oranges
2 tablespoons maple syrup
2 tablespoons Cointreau or Grand Marnier
liqueur
crème fraîche, to serve

SERVES 4

60

I Cut 8 identical squares of foil, each large enough to wrap an orange. Double up the squares for extra strength, then brush the center of each square with a little of the melted butter.

2 Carefully pare the rind from one orange. Using a sharp knife, scrape off any pith, then cut the rind into matchstick strips. Place the rind in a small saucepan, add water to cover and bring to a boil. Cook for 5 minutes, then drain the strips and set them aside.

3 Peel all the oranges, keeping them whole and taking care to remove all the pith. Working over a bowl to catch the juice, slice them horizontally into several thick slices. Reassemble each orange and place it on a square of doubled foil.

4 Tuck the foil around each orange, leaving the foil open at the top. Stir the maple syrup and liqueur into the orange juice, then spoon the mixture over the oranges. Add a dab of butter and close the foil to seal in the juices.

5 Place the packages on a hot barbecue and cook for 10–12 minutes, until hot. Serve with crème fraîche, topped with shreds of blanched orange rind.

COOK'S TIP

For an alcohol-free version of this delicious
dessert, substitute golden marmalade
for the Cointreau or Grand Marnier.

Barbecued Strawberry Croissants

4 croissants
½ cup ricotta cheese
strawberry jam

SERVES 4

62

1 Split the croissants in half and open them on a board. Spread the bottom half of each croissant with ricotta cheese.

2 Top the bottom half of each croissant with a generous spoonful of strawberry jam, spreading it evenly. Replace the top half of each croissant.

3 Place the filled croissants on a hot barbecue and cook for 2–3 minutes, turning once. Serve the croissants immediately, on their own or with ice cream.

VARIATIONS

• Fresh scones or muffins can be toasted on the barbecue as an alternative to croissants.
• Vary the filling. Cream cheese or mascarpone can be used instead of ricotta, and apricot or black cherry jam instead of strawberry.

Fruit Kebabs with Chocolate & Marshmallow Fondue

INGREDIENTS

2 bananas
2 kiwi fruits
12 strawberries
1 tablespoon butter, melted
1 tablespoon lemon juice
1 teaspoon ground cinnamon
FONDUE
½ pound semisweet or bittersweet chocolate, broken into squares
½ cup light cream or half-and-half
8 marshmallows
½ teaspoon vanilla extract

1 Soak 4 bamboo skewers in cold water for 30 minutes. Peel the bananas and cut each one into 4 thick chunks. Peel and quarter the kiwi fruit.

2 Drain the skewers and thread them with the bananas, kiwi fruit and strawberries. Mix the butter, lemon juice and cinnamon in a small bowl and  brush the mixture over the fruit on the skewers.

3 Make the fondue. Combine the chocolate, cream and marshmallows in a small pan. Heat gently on the barbecue, stirring until the mixture has melted and is smooth. Do not allow the mixture to approach the boiling point.

4 Move the fondue to the edge of the barbecue to keep warm. Meanwhile, cook the fruit kebabs for 2–3 minutes, turning once. Stir the vanilla extract into the fondue and serve it with the kebabs.

63

Index